EXTREME
SPORTS
No Limits!

Extreme
Skateboarding

John Crossingham & Bobbie Kalman

 Crabtree Publishing Company

www.crabtreebooks.com

Created by Bobbie Kalman

Dedicated by Rob MacGregor
For Jordan and Evan

Editor-in-Chief
Bobbie Kalman

Writing team
John Crossingham
Bobbie Kalman

Substantive editor
Niki Walker

Project editor
Kelley MacAulay

Editor
Amanda Bishop

Art director
Robert MacGregor

Computer design
Michael Golka
Katherine Kantor

Production coordinator
Heather Fitzpatrick

Photo research
Kelley MacAulay
Laura Hysert

Special thanks to
Mike Armstrong, Ryan Brown, Mike Carr,
Phil Shore, and Shred Central Skatepark

Consultant
Electric Bill Hensley

Photographs
AP/Wide World Photos: pages 6, 8
Marc Crabtree: pages 10, 11 (bottom), 18, 19, 20 (top), 21, 29
Stan Liu: pages 1, 3, 31
Painet Stock Photos: Stew Milne: pages 4, 22
Shazamm: pages 23, 27
Scott Starr: pages 7, 24, 25, 26
Other images by Corbis Images and PhotoDisc

Illustrations
Robert MacGregor: pages 12–13
Margaret Amy Reiach: pages 14–15
Bonna Rouse: page 28

Digital prepress
Embassy Graphics

Printer
Worzalla Publishing Company

Crabtree Publishing Company

www.crabtreebooks.com   1-800-387-7650

PMB 16A
350 Fifth Avenue
Suite 3308
New York, NY
10118

612 Welland Avenue
St. Catharines
Ontario
Canada
L2M 5V6

73 Lime Walk
Headington
Oxford
OX3 7AD
United Kingdom

Cataloging-in-Publication Data
Crossingham, John.
    Extreme skateboarding / John Crossingham & Bobbie Kalman.
        p. cm. -- (Extreme sports no limits series)
Includes index.
Contents: Extreme skateboarding--In the beginning--The next waves--
Skating styles--Meet the board--Skateparks--The fundamentals--
Grind it, slide it--Grab it, flip it--Face off--Legends of the sport--
The new generation -- Dropping in -- Safety first.
    ISBN 0-7787-1668-6 (RLB) -- ISBN 0-7787-1714-3 (pbk.)
    1. Skateboarding--Juvenile literature. 2. Extreme sports--Juvenile
literature. [1. Skateboarding. 2. Extreme sports.] I. Kalman, Bobbie.
II. Title. III. Series.
    GV859.8.C755 2003
    796.22--dc22

2003012910
LC

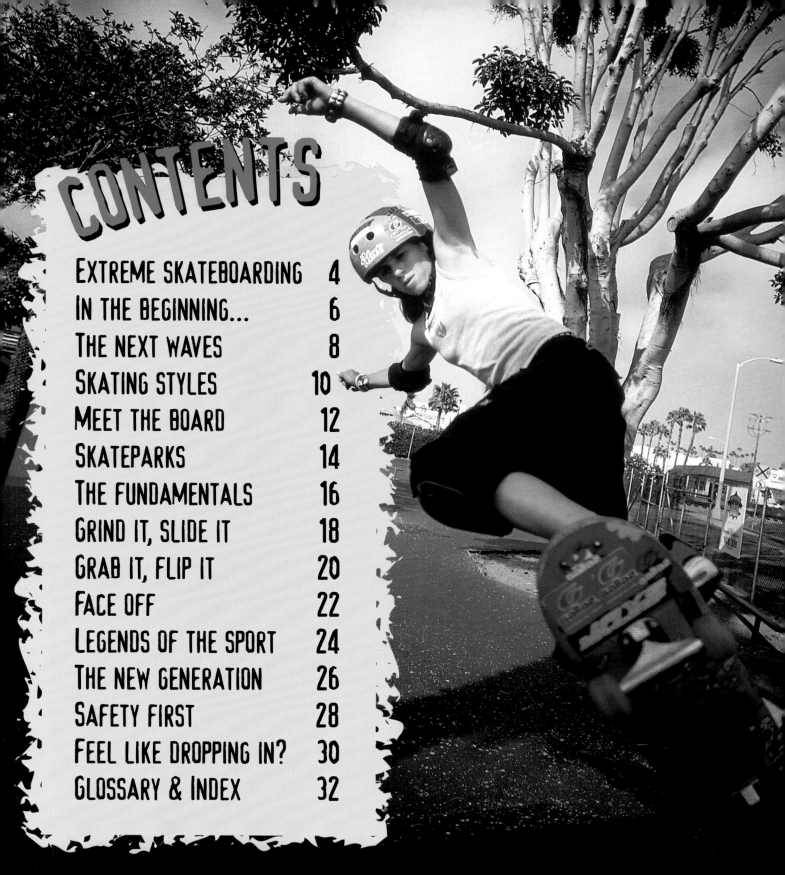

CONTENTS

Extreme skateboarding	4
In the beginning...	6
The next waves	8
Skating styles	10
Meet the board	12
Skateparks	14
The fundamentals	16
Grind it, slide it	18
Grab it, flip it	20
Face off	22
Legends of the sport	24
The new generation	26
Safety first	28
Feel like dropping in?	30
Glossary & Index	32

EXTREME SKATEBOARDING

Skateboarding or "skating" is one of the most popular **individual sports** in the world. In an individual sport, athletes perform alone. Skaters challenge themselves and one another to pull off more and more difficult **tricks**, or moves. A great skater needs balance, strength, timing, coordination, and—most of all—guts!

TAKING IT TO THE EXTREME

For some people, skateboarding is just a fun activity to do after school or in their free time. For serious skaters, however, skateboarding is an **extreme sport**. Extreme sports push athletes to the limits of their abilities. Some extreme skaters are **professionals** or "pros"—they skate for a living. It is their job to be the best skaters they can be. They take the sport to new levels every day. Their ability to master difficult and dangerous tricks is what makes skateboarding an extreme sport.

4

So Cultured

Skateboarding has its own **culture**. A culture is a set of values shared by a group of people. Skating culture includes its own music, clothing, and way of talking. Tricks are given odd names that make sense only to skaters. Certain types of music, such as punk and hip-hop, match an extreme skater's aggressive style. Many pro skaters have started their own skateboard and clothing companies to make boards and gear that appeal to a skater's needs and sense of style.

You Stole My Moves!

Many extreme sports owe a debt to skateboarding. Aggressive in-line skating, wakeboarding, snowboarding, and BMX stunt riding all have tricks that are based on skateboarding moves. The tricks even have the same names. Some skateboarders tour with top in-line skaters and BMX riders to perform stunts and tricks that amaze crowds.

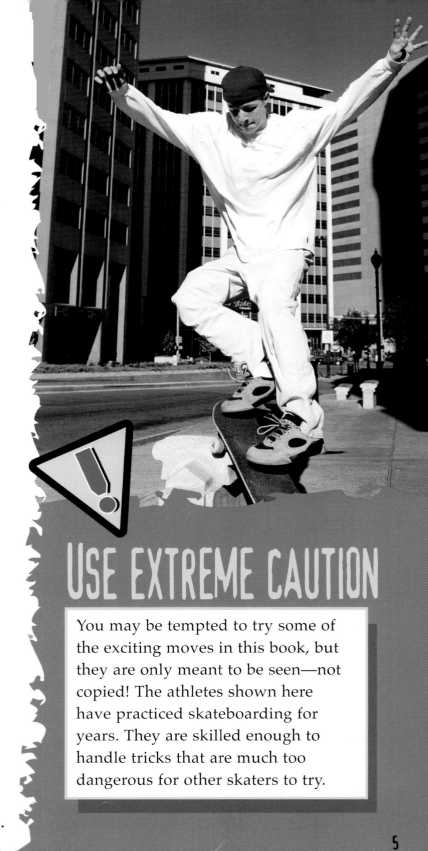

Use Extreme Caution

You may be tempted to try some of the exciting moves in this book, but they are only meant to be seen—not copied! The athletes shown here have practiced skateboarding for years. They are skilled enough to handle tricks that are much too dangerous for other skaters to try.

IN THE BEGINNING...

The first skateboards were homemade contraptions built in the early 1900s, when roller skates and **scooters** were popular. A scooter is a flat board with four wheels on the bottom and a handle attached to the front. Some kids decided scooters would be more fun without the handles. Others took the wheels off their roller skates and attached them to wooden boards. Although these inventions were the first "skateboards," no one called them that yet.

SURFIN' U.S.A.

In the mid 1950s, surfing became very popular in California. Movies and music featured the sport, and a surfing craze swept the United States. Surfing was fun, but most kids lived far from an ocean. In 1959, toy companies began making "surfboards" everyone could use, no matter where they lived. These "sidewalk surfers" were the first factory-made skateboards.

Early skateboards didn't turn easily—some couldn't turn at all! The goal of skating was simply to stay on the board while riding downhill.

TIME LINE:

1950s: surfing craze hits California

early 1900s: roller skates and scooters are popular; early "skateboards" are invented

1959: toy companies make the first skateboards to be sold in stores

6

THAT'S NOT SAFE

Early skateboards had wheels made of metal or clay. These wheels stopped suddenly when they hit small rocks or cracks in pavement. There were no helmets, pads, or other safety equipment for skaters. Parents became concerned because their kids kept getting hurt. By 1965, many cities passed laws making it illegal to ride skateboards on streets or on public property. Stores stopped ordering boards, so companies stopped making them. At the end of the 1960s, it looked as if skateboarding was finished!

THE DIE-HARDS

Although skateboarding became unpopular in the mid 1960s, die-hard skateboarders didn't give up. Boards were difficult to buy, so skaters built their own using scraps of wood and roller-skate wheels. They practiced in back yards, empty swimming pools and streets, and any other space they could find. Skating culture went **underground**, or away from the public.

1966: skating's popularity drops due to bans and poor quality boards

1965: cities begin to ban skateboards

1963: Makaha Skateboards, one of the best skateboard companies of the '60s and '70s, is created

*1969: Larry Stevenson, owner of Makaha, invents the **kicktail** (see page 13)*

early 1960s: skating is popular across America

Metal skateboard wheels, shown above, made early skateboards dangerous because they did not grip pavement well.

THE NEXT WAVES

Early tricks often involved balancing on the board. The handstand was a popular move in the early '70s.

In 1970, Frank Nasworthy changed skating forever. He used a plastic called **urethane** to make new skateboard wheels. These wheels glided over bumps and didn't slide the way metal wheels did. Specially designed skating **trucks**, or wheel bases, were also invented. These inventions made boards safer, smoother, faster, and easier to turn. Skating started to make a comeback.

IT'S GETTING BETTER!

The years between 1973 and 1980 are known as the **Second Wave** in skating. **Skateparks** were built as places just for skating. New boards allowed skaters to be more daring than ever. The best of these inventive skaters were the **Z-boys** from an area of Santa Monica, California, called Dogtown (see page 24). Everyone copied their aggressive style, and extreme skateboarding was born!

8

THIRD TIME'S A CHARM

Skateboarding's popularity exploded again during the **Third Wave**, which lasted from 1983 to 1991. During this time, skating became more difficult as pros invented new tricks and altered old tricks. The sport also became part of **pop culture**. Skaters appeared in rock videos, commericals, magazines, and TV shows, and skating reached its largest audience yet.

HERE TO STAY

Skating's popularity crashed briefly in the early 1990s, but the **Fourth Wave** began a couple of years later and has been going strong ever since. Along with aggressive in-line skating and BMX, skateboarding has launched an extreme-sports boom around the world. There are now more pros, competitions, and skateparks than ever before.

TIME LINE:

1981: Thrasher *magazine is first published*

1983: Third Wave begins

1970: urethane skateboard wheels are invented

*1980: Second Wave ends due to safety concerns and poor sales; the **Bones Brigade** is formed (see page 24)*

*1984: **vertical** skating becomes the leading style (see page 10)*

1972: the Cadillac Wheel is the first commercial urethane wheel sold

mid 1980s: skate videos and skate fashions become popular with kids

1976: first skateparks open in Florida and California

1973: Second Wave begins

*1993 to present: Fourth Wave of skating inspires **X Games**, video games, etc.*

*late 1980s: **street** skating becomes the main style (see page 11)*

1975: "Z-boys" pro skate team is formed

1974: a new truck made by Tracker Trucks improves turning

1991: poor sales end the Third Wave

9

SKATING STYLES

Over the past forty years, skating has changed and grown as a sport. Skaters living in different areas developed their own **styles** of skating. Over time, two main skating styles have emerged—vertical or "vert" and street. Vert and street have more in common than it may appear—both styles use many of the same tricks. Each style uses different **obstacles**, or objects, for performing tricks.

VERT SKATING

Vert skating is all about "getting vertical," or flying up in the air. Vert skating began in empty swimming pools in the '70s. Skaters found they could build a lot of speed by **carving** up and down a pool's sloping sides. Soon, skaters were flying above the edges of the pools and developing new tricks. These tricks, done in midair, are known as **aerials**. Today, vert skaters use pools, **pipe ramps**, and **bowls** to build speed and get air.

STREET SKATING

Street skating is done—you guessed it—on streets. The street is where skating was born, and it's still a big part of the sport. Street skaters perform a wide variety of tricks on common obstacles, including benches, railings, curbs, stairs, and just about any other sturdy structure found on the street.

FEELING FREE

In **freestyle** or **flatland** skating, skaters do not use obstacles or ramps. Instead, they perform balancing and **flip** tricks on flat pavement. Freestyle hit its peak in popularity in the mid 1970s, when skaters were starting to define the sport and push the limits of the new boards. Since they did not use obstacles, freestyle skaters had to be very creative. Freestyle's popularity dropped in the '80s and '90s, but street skaters took many of the tricks, such as the **manual**, shown left, and brought them to street obstacles. Today, freestyle is generally a part of street skating.

MEET THE

*Trucks **pivot**, or turn, around the kingpin. They allow a skater to turn by simply leaning to one side or the other.*

kingpin

Artwork is a big part of skateboarding culture. Skaters can buy boards already covered with eye-catching art, or they can decorate their boards themselves.

A skateboard is made up of three main sections —the **deck**, the trucks, and the wheels. Each plays a part in the speed, weight, and **maneuverability** of the skateboard. In the past, there were boards for street skating and boards for vert skating. Today, most boards aren't designed for one style or the other. They're made to handle whatever style skaters want to try.

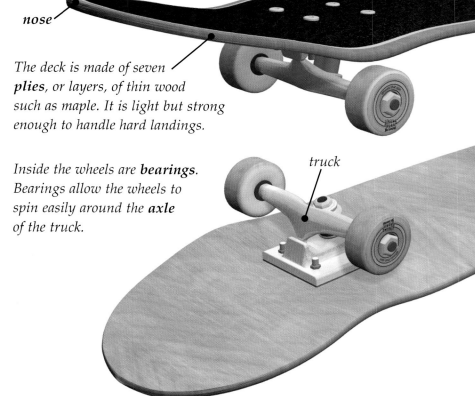

nose

*The deck is made of seven **plies**, or layers, of thin wood such as maple. It is light but strong enough to handle hard landings.*

*Inside the wheels are **bearings**. Bearings allow the wheels to spin easily around the **axle** of the truck.*

truck

BOARD

The surface of a board is covered by black **grip tape**, which is gritty like sandpaper.

kicktail

The sides of the deck are called **rails**.

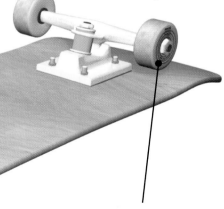

Wheels are still made of urethane because it is a durable material that grips well. Since the '90s, wheels have become smaller. Small wheels are good for street skating and performing common tricks.

ALL DECKED OUT

The first decks were short and skinny. As skating developed and styles changed through the '70s and '80s, deck designs became more and more inventive. Today's decks can be traced back to the street deck designs of the '90s.

In the 1970s, decks were made from all sorts of materials, including plastic, wood, and fiberglass. The kicktail became a standard feature and made a whole new world of tricks possible.

Vert decks used by Tony Hawk and Christian Hosoi in the '80s were wide and often had a slight fish shape, as shown above.

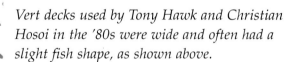

The decks of '80s freestyle masters such as Rodney Mullen and Per Welinder were much slimmer than vert decks. The freestyle models had a curved nose and tail and straight sides. Through the '90s, all decks moved closer to the freestyle model, becoming lighter and easier to flip.

SKATEPARKS

The biggest problem with skating on the street is that skaters can get in the way of pedestrians or cars—and it's often illegal! Skateparks give skaters safer places to practice. They provide an escape from the everyday world. Challenges lie around every corner, and the only traffic is other skaters. Today's skateparks have tons of street and vert obstacles, such as railings, **fun boxes**, **mini ramps**, pipe ramps, and bowls.

PIPE DREAMS

Pipe ramps are the giants of skatepark obstacles. They have curved sloping sides called **transitions**. A **half-pipe** has two transitions facing each other. A **quarter-pipe** has one transition. Skaters ride up and down transitions to gain speed and height. A ramp's edge is known as the **coping** or **lip**. Pipe ramps are made with specially treated plywood that is very strong.

Fun boxes are small raised platforms that have two or four sloping sides. Some fun boxes also have obstacles such as railings for performing street tricks.

Mini ramps have small curved transitions. They allow street skaters to get some air quickly, but not as much air as vert skaters get from pipe ramps.

Skateparks often have rounded pools called bowls. Here, skaters can perform vert tricks or carve up and down the sloping sides.

15

THE FUNDAMENTALS

Pro skaters can seem like magicians. They have hundreds of tricks to choose from, and new tricks are invented all the time. Strange names like "benihana" and "lien" make these tricks even more mystifying to non-skaters, but all magicians have a secret. For skaters, that secret is the **ollie**. Along with a few other basic tricks, it's a fundamental of skating.

LOOK MA, NO RAMP!

"Ollie" was the nickname of the trick's creator, Alan Gelfand. He discovered that by kicking down on the board's tail and jumping up, he could make the skateboard stay with his feet as he popped up off the ground. The ollie changed how everyone skated. Skaters no longer needed ramps to get some air. Today, the ollie is still the most important move in skateboarding. It's the starting point of almost every other trick skaters perform.

Skaters always try to ollie over higher and higher obstacles. Pylons and fire hydrants are popular street ollie obstacles. Even vert skaters ollie at the coping to get extra air.

AROUND AND AROUND

Spins are a type of aerial trick. They test a skater's sense of direction and balance. In the air, skaters turn themselves and their boards around before landing. Spins are named for the number of degrees a skater turns. A full turn is called a **360** because there are 360° in a circle. A half-turn is called a **180**.

*Many pros can perform a **540**, or a full turn and a half. Some can even manage a **720**—two full turns—in midair!*

BODY TALK

Skaters have a whole set of words that they use to describe their body positions. Here are a few of the most common terms:

*Regular: the **stance**, or body position, with the right foot on the tail and the left foot on the nose*
Goofy: the opposite stance of regular—left foot on the tail, right foot on the nose (goofy is the normal stance for most lefties)
Frontside: the side of the board a skater's chest normally faces
Backside: the side of the board a skater's back usually faces
Fakie: when a skater rides backwards in his or her normal stance
*Switch or **switchstance**: riding in the stance that is the opposite of a skater's natural stance (when a regular skater rides goofy, he or she has "switched")*
Nollie: an ollie that is done by kicking the nose instead of the tail ("nollie" is short for "nose ollie")
*Manual: balancing on the back wheels while moving; a **nose manual** is done when a skater balances on the front wheels*

GRIND IT, SLIDE IT

Once a skater knows how to ollie, he or she can leap onto an obstacle and perform a **grind** or **slide** trick. In these tricks, the skater skids along the obstacle. Balance is important—otherwise the skater falls. Grinds and slides are a huge part of street skating. The tricks are done on obstacles such as railings and benches. Vert skaters also grind and slide, but they perform the tricks on a ramp's coping.

*Grinding both trucks at once is called a **50-50**.*

GRINDS

To do a grind trick, a skater scrapes the board's trucks along an obstacle. The grind gets its name from the grinding sound the metal trucks make as they drag on the obstacle's surface. Grinds require excellent balance and good speed, or the skater will fall off the obstacle.

*A **crooked grind** is done on an angle using both the front truck and the deck's nose.*

SLIDES

A slide is like a grind, but a skater skids over the obstacle on the board's deck instead of on the trucks. Slides are usually named for the part of the deck that touches the obstacle, as in **boardslides**, **tailslides**, and **noseslides**.

LIP SERVICE

For vert skaters, grinds and slides are also known as **lip tricks** because they are done on the lip of the ramp. **Stalls** are another type of lip trick. In a stall, a skater stops the board briefly on the lip by balancing on the board's tail or a truck. The **rock 'n' roll** and **disaster** are types of stalls. Another lip trick is the **handplant**, shown above—a one-handed handstand that demands great balance!

*A boardslide is also known as a **railslide**.*

GRAB IT, FLIP IT

A skater's ability is pushed even further by **grab** and flip tricks. These tricks require skilled coordination of a skater's eyes, hands, and feet. Both vert and street skaters use grabs and flips during their aerials. By adding them to grinds, slides, and spins, skaters can make their tricks even more difficult—and impressive.

Grab tricks require a skater to be flexible and quick.

FLIPS

These quick tricks turn a board wheels-over-deck. Flip tricks require a lot of practice because the board leaves a skater's feet completely. The skater then has to find it before landing! Street skaters use more flip tricks than vert skaters do because flips work well after doing an ollie or grinding a railing.

*To do a **kickflip**, a skater flips the board end over end by pushing down on the rail of the deck with his or her toe.*

GRABS

Grab tricks look like aerial ballet. A skater bends and twists to hold the deck while flying through the air. Some basic grabs, such as the **nosegrab** or **tailgrab**, are named for the part of the deck that's grabbed. Vert skating involves a lot of grab tricks. Vert skaters have more time to hold these tricks than street skaters do because they gain so much air off their ramps.

*The **melon** is a type of grab. The skater grabs the backside rail with the backside hand.*

WHAT'S THE COMBINATION?

When skaters want to challenge themselves, they combine tricks into a **combo**. For example, a skater can make a combo by doing a 180 while doing a melon. Combos can also be made up of a few tricks done in a row. A 50-50 on a railing followed by a kickflip when coming off the railing is a combo.

21

FACE OFF

Vert and street competitions are held all over the world. Competitions test skaters' skills and their devotion to the sport. They also give skaters a chance to show off in front of an audience and push themselves to be creative. Being inventive impresses judges and can score skaters major points.

RUN FOR IT

In most competitions, each skater does two **runs**. A run is a series of tricks and combos. It usually lasts between thirty seconds and one minute. A skater's best run is the one that counts. Skaters usually perform runs alone, but in some events—such as **doubles vert**—two skaters perform together.

PASSING JUDGMENT

Judges score each run out of 100, based on how impressed they are by the performance. They consider factors such as originality, difficulty, smoothness, and use of combos.

*When a skater takes off from one ramp and lands on another ramp, the move is called a **transfer**.*

HITTING THE ROAD

The world's best skaters travel the globe as part of the **pro circuit**. The circuit is a series of skating events held in different cities. The winners often walk away with cash prizes. Sometimes pro tours are held just to promote the sport.

LEGENDS OF THE SPORT

Skateboarding has had its share of **pioneers**—daring skaters who were creative and brave enough to try new tricks and explore new terrain with their boards. Some of these athletes still skate professionally today. Others just skate in their free time. All have left their marks on the sport by pushing it—and themselves—to the limit.

THE Z-BOYS

In 1975, a surfboard and skateboard company called Zephyr formed a pro skate team—the Z-boys—that reinvented skating. They helped invent vert, and their aggressive style eventually led to street skating. This historic team included Stacy Peralta, Peggy Oki, Jay Adams, and the incredible Tony Alva. Alva started his own skateboard company, Alva Skates, when he was nineteen. Peralta formed Powell-Peralta Skates, the biggest skate company of the 1980s.

THE BONES BRIGADE

The Powell-Peralta pro team, The Bones Brigade, was the Z-boys team of the '80s. The team blew away competitors around the world and appeared in some of the very first skate videos. Its members included Tony Hawk, Mike McGill, Lance Mountain, and Steve Caballero, shown above left. Now, in his forties, Caballero still skates. His signature trick, the **Caballaerial**, is a 360 aerial in a fakie stance.

RODNEY MULLEN

In the '80s, Rodney Mullen changed forever how people thought about freestyle tricks. He flipped, balanced, and spun his board as if it were on a string. He invented and named more tricks than most skaters even try to perform. The smooth **darkslide**, done by sliding the top of the deck along an obstacle, is just one of his creations. Unlike many skaters from the '80s, Mullen has remained a force in competition right up to today.

TONY HAWK

Tony Hawk, shown above, is the Wayne Gretzky or Michael Jordan of skating. Before he was a teenager, young Hawk was dazzling pros with his vert skills. For over twenty years, he has helped bring skating to a larger audience. There's even a video game named after him. His greatest legacy remains being the first skater ever to land a **900**—a spin that's two-and-a-half turns!

CHRISTIAN HOSOI

Along with Hawk, Christian Hosoi was another vert superstar in the '80s. His signature "hammerhead" boards were the most popular decks in the 1980s. He is known for getting incredible air on a ramp and is renowned for amazing vert skills.

25

THE NEW GENERATION

Today's pro skaters have a lot to prove. Legends such as Mullen and Hawk are still pushing the limits, but rising stars aren't intimidated. They are inspired to take the sport even further than their heroes have taken it. Some of today's stars use their technical skills to refine and improve complex flip and grind tricks. Others are so courageous that they'll go where no other skater dares to go. Their feats prove that there is a lot of skating history still to be written.

CHAD MUSKA

No one can leap massive flights of stairs or grind railings like this incredible street master. Chad Muska is almost as well known for his outrageous personality as he is for his skating. He produces hip-hop music and wears outfits that always attract attention!

DAEWON SONG

Some skaters go for power, but this Korean skater uses his finesse and skill to impress. Many think Daewon Song is the best technical skater since Rodney Mullen. In fact, they go head-to-head in a video called *Rodney Mullen vs. Daewon Song*!

BOB BURNQUIST

Think switchstance tricks are difficult? If Brazilian skater Bob Burnquist ever did, he's not telling anyone about it. Burnquist is a vert skater who rivals even the great Tony Hawk. He is incredible at skating in his switchstance. He was the first to perform his signature trick, the **Burntwist**.

KAREEM CAMPBELL

Born in New York, Kareem Campbell began his career as a vert skater. Today, he lives in Los Angeles, where he eats and breathes street skating. Campbell is a good example of today's extreme street skater—no move is too difficult for him to conquer. He owns a skate company, Axion Footwear, and a record store.

ELYSSA STEAMER

This Florida native is one of the greatest street skaters to hit the deck. Her fearless style is an inspiration for girls in a sport that is often seen as a boys' club—in fact, Elyssa Steamer is the only girl to make it into Tony Hawk's video game!

SAFETY FIRST

During the '60s, '70s, and '80s, skateboarding was constantly under fire from parents who complained that their kids were getting hurt. One of the reasons skating has grown is that safety equipment has improved. Before any skater heads to the park, putting on proper equipment is a must! The most important piece of equipment is a helmet—no one should ever skate without one.

Safe skaters also wear knee pads, elbow pads, and wrist pads. Proper pads and a good helmet are a must—the pros never compete without them.

*A skating helmet is lightweight but strong. The outside **shell** is hard plastic. Inside is a soft foam lining that cushions the head. The **chin strap** should always be well fastened.*

Elbow pads and knee pads have hard plastic shells for protection. Most fasten with Velcro straps.

Gloves will help save fingers from nasty scrapes and cuts.

A good pair of skate shoes helps keep a skater safe by supporting the ankles.

FANCY FOOTWEAR

Skate shoes are very popular—many people who wear them don't even skate! All skate shoes are lightweight, with grip-pattern rubber soles and good ankle support. Vans and Airwalk are the granddaddies of skating footwear, but Etnies and DC make footwear that is just as popular among skaters today.

GOING DOWN?

Bails, or falls, are a fact of life, even for pro skaters. When skaters bail, they focus on preventing injuries to themselves—the board can handle the fall! The **knee-slide**, shown here, is a simple way to bail on a ramp or bowl. If a grind or a slide goes badly, a skater usually just jumps away from the obstacle.

A LITTLE RESPECT

Skating is about attitude, but it is also about respect. In a crowded skatepark, skaters wait their turns. After a few runs in a bowl, they come to the top and allow other skaters to strut their stuff. Waiting their turn helps them avoid nasty collisions. They also watch other skaters and try to learn from their tricks— and their mistakes!

Skaters only get as much respect from other skaters as they give.

FEEL LIKE DROPPING IN ?

Watching pros perform impossible stunts with nothing but a deck and four wheels is very inspiring. If you feel like picking up your own board after reading this book, good for you! One of the best things about skating is that you can do it just about anywhere and learn at your own speed. Just remember that the incredible moves you saw in this book are for pros only—not beginners. One of the best and safest ways to improve as a skater is to find a coach or **mentor** to help guide you at your own pace.

READ ABOUT IT

The best resources for learning about skating are magazines dedicated to the sport. Mags started in the '80s, like *Thrasher* and *Transworld Skateboarding*, are still going strong, and there are many others today. All feature trick tips, interviews with pros, and a lot of great shots. For more great info, try a web search or check out these websites:

www.skateboarding.com - Transworld Skateboarding's site
www.exploratorium.edu/skateboarding - cool definitions and scientific explanations
expn.go.com - site devoted to all extreme sports and the X Games
www.switchmagazine.com - an online skate magazine with tips, reviews, and links

PURCHASING POWER

When you are looking for a board, shop around. Avoid the cheap stuff, but don't buy the most expensive equipment either. You won't impress anyone with a hip board unless you know how to use it! A good skate shop employee can help you find a starter board that's suited to your skill level.

HOT SPOTS

With its sunny weather and loads of skateparks, California is the skating capital of the world. Large cities like New York are also great for street skaters to explore. Quality skateparks are found everywhere from Oregon to Florida. A hot spot could be just around the corner!

GLOSSARY

Note: Boldfaced words that are defined in the book may not appear in the glossary.

axle A small metal bar around which skateboard wheels revolve

bearing A part of a skateboard wheel that allows the wheel to rotate smoothly

bowl A round, sunken structure at a skatepark

carve To skate around the walls inside a bowl

coping The edge of a ramp

disaster A stall trick performed by dropping onto a ramp's edge

flip A trick done by flipping the skateboard wheels-over-deck

kicktail The upturned angle on the end of a skateboard

maneuverability The capability of a skateboard to be moved smoothly and effectively by a skater

mentor An experienced person who can provide advice and assistance

ollie A trick done by popping the skateboard off the ground

pipe ramp A giant ramp with curved sloping sides used in vert skating

pop culture The music, movies, and fashion commonly known by the general public

rock 'n' roll A stall trick done by balancing the center of the board on the edge of a ramp

skatepark An indoor or outdoor park full of obstacles on which skaters can practice

style A particular type of skating, such as vert or street

urethane A hard plastic used to make modern skateboard wheels

X Games A series of extreme sports competitions sponsored by ESPN

INDEX

bails 29
Bones Brigade 9, 24
bowls 10, 14, 15, 29
competitions 9, 22–23
culture 5, 7, 9
freestyle 11, 13, 25
fun boxes 14, 15

half-pipe 14
mini ramps 14, 15
pipe ramps 10, 14, 15
quarter-pipe 14
safety 5, 7, 28–29
skateparks 8, 9, 14–15, 29, 31

street 9, 10, 11, 12, 13, 14, 15, 16, 18, 20, 21, 22, 24, 26, 27, 31
tricks 4, 5, 8, 9, 10, 11, 13, 15, 16, 17, 18, 19, 20, 21, 24, 25, 27
vert 9, 10, 12, 13, 14, 15, 16, 18, 19, 20, 21, 22, 24, 25, 27
Z-boys 9, 24

1 2 3 4 5 6 7 8 9 0 Printed in the U.S.A. 3 2 1 0 9 8 7 6 5 4